WHEN YOUR
PRAYERS
Seem
Unanswered

S. MICHAEL WILCOX

DESERET
BOOK

SALT LAKE CITY, UTAH

Visit us at deseretbook.com

Library of Congress Cataloging-in-Publication Data
Wilcox, S. Michael.
    When your prayers seem unanswered / S. Michael Wilcox.
    p.   cm.
    Includes bibliographical references and index.
    ISBN-10 1-59038-586-1 (hardbound : alk. paper)
    ISBN-13 978-1-59038-586-9 (hardbound : alk. paper)
    1. Mormon women—Religious life.   2. Prayer—Mormon
Church.   I. Title.
    BX8641.W54   2006
    248.8'43—dc22   2006006523

Printed in Mexico
R. R. Donnelley and Sons, Reynosa, Mexico

10   9   8   7   6   5   4

LETTERS FROM FATHER

A NUMBER OF YEARS AGO my eldest daughter
went to Russia. This was before e-mail was
the popular and convenient means of communica-
tion it has become. Russia was just opening up to
the world, and she was going to teach English in
Moscow. Our ability to communicate with her
would be intermittent at best, and we were concerned about her welfare. In order for us to sup-
port her at such a long distance I decided to write
some letters before she went just in case we
couldn't talk to her during her six-month stay. She
was just out of high school, and as a parent, I was
somewhat concerned. I tried to imagine every
problem, dilemma, emotion, concern, feeling of
loneliness, elation (from the high to the low), she
might experience in that time period. I then wrote

a letter of counsel, comfort, or advice that she could read there, since I couldn't otherwise readily communicate with her. I labeled each letter on the outside: "When You're Discouraged"; "When You Get Homesick"; "When You Are Tempted"; and so forth. During our good-byes at the airport, I handed her the large packet of letters that I hoped would aid her in solving any concerns she might have.

I was not omniscient about everything she would face during those six months, but I did hit a number of them. Some of the letters she opened after her return home, just to see what I had written, even though she hadn't faced that particular concern.

I believe there is a parallel to this situation in all of our lives. In a manner of speaking, the scriptures are like a handful of letters from our Father in Heaven, who has anticipated the questions and concerns we might have from time to time during our mortal existence. Unlike me, he knows *all* the varied and multiple experiences his children will face, and so he has provided answers for us before we even ask the questions, face the temptations, or are challenged by life's trials.

During many years of teaching, I have been asked a number of questions, but one stands above the rest because of how often it has been asked and the number of different age groups that have shared its concern. It is sometimes phrased in different words, but the theme is essentially the same: "How do I get answers to prayer?" "Why does the Lord deal with us the way he deals with us?" "Why, sometimes, do we appear not to get answers at all?" "Why do others receive their desires and I do not?" "How can I know the answers are coming from God and not from my own mind?"

Maybe if I describe the details of an extreme case it will cover everything to a lesser degree. The scriptures do tend to deal with extremes for that very reason.

"DID HEAVEN LOOK ON?"

THERE ARE TWO LINES FROM Shakespeare I often quote to myself when I face certain dilemmas in life. I repeat, these represent extreme situations, but they quite succinctly state the difficulty most of us face. Here are the quotes. The first is from *The Tragedy of King Richard III*. Elizabeth, who is the dispossessed former queen, receives word that the two princes, her two young sons, have been executed in the Tower of London by their uncle, Richard III. She raises her eyes to heaven and prays:

> *Wilt thou, O God, fly from such gentle lambs,*
> *And throw them in the entrails of the wolf?*
> *When didst thou sleep when such a deed was done?*
> (Act IV, Scene iv)

The second quote is from *The Tragedy of Macbeth.*
Macduff learns that Macbeth has killed Macduff's
entire family. Once again, there is a turning to
heaven and a wondering and a questioning why
there was not help in such a desperate situation.
Macduff in his agony cries:

> *Did heaven look on,*
> *And would not take their part?*
> (Act IV, Scene iii)

In lesser moments in my life—and perhaps in
lesser moments in your life—I must admit I am
sometimes tempted to be critical of the way that
God is running the universe, at least our corner of
it. I have a tendency occasionally to look heavenward and quote Shakespeare, and say as Macduff
said, "Did heaven look on, and would not take
their part?"

The issue at hand is not always one concerning
my own desires or needs. It often occurs when I see
someone I love seemingly denied righteous long-
ings or called to endure life's trials beyond reason.
On a broader scope, even a cursory perusal of the

nightly news can provide sufficient fodder for a heavenward glance and a quiet quoting of Macduff.

I think about a daughter who was born wanting to be a mother but who hasn't yet been able to have children; another daughter longing to be married who just turned thirty-two and still hasn't had that joy in her life; a wife who, in spite of blessings and prayers and temple rolls, lives in pain everyday. And these are just some of the concerns in the great ocean of human experience. I'm convinced all of us have those disappointing, trying times when we wonder why "heaven [looks] on, and [will] not take [our] part."

THE FOURTH
WATCH

I WOULD LIKE TO SUGGEST some things that go through my mind in those difficult moments of life. Hopefully they'll be of value to you as they have been to me. They are the letters I peruse from a kind Father in Heaven, who knew beforehand we would face such dilemmas and questions. One of the first of those scriptural letters contains a principle I call "The Fourth Watch."

A New Testament day was divided into twelve hours, beginning at six in the morning. The third hour would be nine o'clock, the sixth hour would be noon, and the eleventh hour, though we visualize it as being just before midnight, actually was five o'clock in the evening. The night was divided into four watches: The first watch was from six in the evening until nine at night. The second watch was nine until midnight, the third watch from midnight until three in the morning, and the fourth watch from three in the morning until six, about sunrise.

The Savior had just fed the five thousand. He instructed his disciples to get into a boat and pick him up later, after he had dismissed the multitude and later spent some solitude in prayer. The disciples obeyed. It was late afternoon or early evening when they got into the ship and pushed out into the Sea of Galilee. Jesus sent the multitude home and then turned to communion with his Father. He prayed into the evening and long into the night.

In the meantime, a storm had swept down on the disciples in their voyage: "And when even was come, the ship was in the midst of the sea, and he alone on the land. And he saw them toiling in rowing; for the wind was contrary unto them" (Mark 6:47–48). In Matthew's version it says, "The ship was . . . tossed with waves" (Matthew 14:24), and in John's account we read: "And the sea arose by reason of a great wind that blew. So when they had

rowed about five and twenty or thirty furlongs . . ."
(John 6:18–19).

A furlong is about 220 to 225 yards. So if they
have rowed 25 to 30 furlongs, they've rowed about
65 to 70 football fields, into the wind during the
storm. As would be expected, they are exhausted
and fearful. Mark's version adds one tiny little
point that the others don't, something I think is
really important. Mark relates that Jesus "saw them
toiling in rowing" (Mark 6:48). They did not know
that he was aware of their danger. They didn't realize he was up on the hill looking down watching
them. They only knew that they had rowed a long
time, the wind remaining contrary, that they were
exhausted, and that they needed help.

And then we read: "About *the fourth watch* of the
night he cometh unto them, walking upon the sea,
. . . [and] they . . . saw him, and were troubled. And
immediately he talked with them, and saith unto
them, Be of good cheer: it is I; be not afraid. And
he went up unto them into the ship; and the wind
ceased" (Mark 6:48–51; emphasis added).

I have a feeling that the Apostles, if they could
have chosen, would have had the Lord come in an

earlier watch. I put it to you, as I frequently put it to myself—when I toil in rowing against the wind, when the sea arises and I'm frightened and it's dark and the storm keeps blowing, and I want help—I want him to come in the *first* watch. I'm a first-watch type of a person. Aren't we all?

But there is also something inside of me that channels my thinking to the realization that it is good to toil in rowing against the wind—that there's something to be gained by exercising spiritual muscles that are stretched in facing trials and opposition. All right, we can accept that. But if he doesn't come in the first watch he certainly ought to come in the second watch. However, it appears that we worship a "fourth-watch" God. And it is important for us to *realize* that we worship a fourth-watch God.

Sometimes I pray: "Lord, I know you're a fourth-watch God and that I'm a first-watch person. Couldn't we compromise and have you come at the end of the second watch or at the beginning of the third watch? Wouldn't that be fair?" But the compromise rarely comes, and in my better moments I know it's good that it doesn't. He's a fourth-watch God.

There are a number of scriptures that help us understand that he truly is a fourth-watch God. Take Joseph Smith's experience, for instance. Doesn't this sound like a fourth-watch response? "At *the very moment when I was ready to sink into despair* and abandon myself to destruction—. . . *just at this moment of great alarm,* I saw a pillar of light exactly over my head" (JS—H 1:16; emphasis added). The Lord tends to come at the moment of great alarm, when we're "ready to sink into despair."

The story of Hagar in Genesis 21 contains a wonderful "fourth-watch" phrase in describing her desperation: "The water was spent in the bottle" (Genesis 21:15). She was out wandering in the wilderness of Beer-sheba with her son, Ishmael, when "she cast the child under one of the shrubs. And she went, and sat her down over against him a good way off, as it were a bowshot: for she said, Let me not see the death of the child. And she sat over against him, and lift up her voice, and wept. And God heard the voice of the lad; and the angel of God called to Hagar out of heaven, and said unto her, What aileth thee, Hagar? fear not; for God hath heard the voice of the lad where he is. Arise, lift up the lad, and hold him in thine hand; . . . And God opened her eyes, and she saw a well of water; and she went, and filled the bottle with water, and gave the lad drink" (Genesis 21:15–19).

God often comes to us when "the water [is] spent in the bottle," then shows us the previously undiscovered, life-giving waters of the nearby well.

In 1 Kings 17, another widow, desperate in a time of famine, does not know help is just around the corner when Elijah meets her at the gate. The prophet directs her: "Bring me, I pray thee, a morsel of bread in thine hand. And she said, As the Lord thy God liveth, I have not a cake, but an handful of meal in a barrel, and a little oil in a cruse: and, behold, I am gathering two sticks, that I may go in and dress it for me and my son, that we may eat it, and die" (1 Kings 17:11–12).

Elijah appears just at the moment she is gathering those two pathetic tiny sticks for the last meal. When the water is spent in the bottle; at the moment of despair; when we're preparing the last meal, that's when the Lord tends to come.

When we advance into the second watch and he doesn't come, a certain cold fear often begins to spread through us as the wind's velocity does not diminish. As we move into the third watch we may be tempted to make some assumptions that are very dangerous and foolish to make. "God is not listening to me." "He doesn't care." Or, more dangerous yet, "He is not there." At times the universe can seem so very empty—all that dark space filled with cold stars. Or, very common to Latter-day Saints, we assume, "I'm not worthy." "He's not listening." "He doesn't care." "No one is there to respond." Because if he were there and if he were listening or if I were worthy, he would certainly come.

When you feel somewhat desperate, when it seems like your prayers aren't answered and the winds still blow, take comfort in the knowledge that he is on the hillside watching. Remember, you might not know that he's watching as you struggle in the boat, but he is on the hillside watching, and he *will* come. But he generally comes in the fourth watch—after we have done all we can do.

TIGHT LIKE
A DISH

OCCASIONALLY I HAVE TOLD that story, shared that principle, and I've had people come up afterwards and say, "You know, I'm sure I'm past the fourth watch. I think I'm in the seventh, or the eighth, or the ninth watch, and he still hasn't come." We need another letter from the Father, for without doubt he foresaw just such extremities. There is another principle that applies in such cases. For those times when I've reached my fourth watch and he hasn't come, then I say these words to myself: *My ship is tight like a dish!*

In Ether we read of storms and mountainous waves that threaten to sink the Jaredite barges and immerse their inhabitants in a salty grave. I'm an English major, and I tend to subconsciously edit just about everything I read. When I read the scriptures I am often very impressed by the beauty of their language and the depth of their truths, but occasionally I come across a verse where I think, *Lord, this could be stated a little better.* I used to read Ether 2:17 and find it hard to resist the temptation to edit it. If I were an English teacher assessing the account of the Jaredite crossing, I would put a red line through Ether 2:17, accompanied by the word *redundant.*

This is the description of the barges that the brother of Jared (Moriancumer) was instructed to build: "They were built after a manner that they were exceedingly tight, even that they would hold water *like unto a dish.*" Point made: they're waterproof. But notice how the author seems to belabor that point: "And the bottom thereof was *tight like unto a dish;* and the sides thereof were *tight like unto a dish;* and the ends thereof were peaked; and the top thereof was *tight like unto a dish;* and the length thereof was the length of a tree; and the door thereof, when it was shut, was *tight like unto a dish*" (Ether 2:17; emphasis added).

As I say, in my weaker moments of intellectual insight, I used to criticize that description. It took me a while to realize that God knows what he's doing in his scriptures, and there is one thing he wants us to understand about that ship—and he *really* wants us to understand it—and that is: "It is tight like a dish." It isn't going to sink! If I really grasp that truth, the application to life is powerful.

The brother of Jared discovers two problems with the boats he is constructing: 1. They lack oxygen; no one can breathe in them. 2. They are so dark inside the pilot cannot see to steer the ship. (Maybe it was Mrs. Moriancumer who pointed out those two defects: "Are you sure, dear, that you got the barge instructions right? Maybe we should check the blueprints again.") The narrative seems to suggest that God designed the ships; and I think he designed them in a way to teach Moriancumer and, through Moriancumer, all of us some great principles.

The brother of Jared climbed a mountain and asked the Lord for solutions. The Lord instructed him to cut some holes that could be blocked when the waves washed over the deck and buried the ship underwater. This would solve the problem of air. But he left the solution of light and steerage to Moriancumer to figure out. He did give him some parameters to work within: "Ye cannot have windows, for they will be dashed in pieces; neither shall ye take fire with you, for ye shall not go by the light of fire" (Ether 2:23).

The Lord has a pretty good sense of humor, I think. I can just see him saying: *No light, no air? I can't imagine how I missed that in the design, but let's see, how about windows? No, no, that won't work; you know waves would break them. How about fire? No, no, that won't work; oxygen is a problem anyway, and with all the pitching and rolling of the ship, fire would be a hazard. Difficult predicament. You figure something out.*

Then the Lord says something that is really amazing to me. Put yourself in Moriancumer's position—you get to solve the problem, right? Tell me what solution you would come up with when the Lord says this: "Behold, ye shall be as a whale in the midst of the sea; for the mountain waves shall dash upon you." Now, let's pause for a second. What causes mountain waves in the ocean? Wind. Wind creates waves and storms, hurricanes, and tempests. Then the Lord explains: "Nevertheless, I will bring you up again out of the depths of the sea" (Ether 2:24). The mountain waves are going to crash over the boat and submerge it for a while and then it will bob up again. They're not submarines. They'll come up to the surface again, but there will be times when the waves wash over the top and everything will be underwater.

Then the Lord makes this remarkable statement: "For the winds have gone forth out of my mouth, and also the rains and the floods have I sent forth" (Ether 2:24).

What solution would you offer to God at that point? This would be my reply: "Lord, we don't have a quandary with air or light at all in these boats. If waves are the problem and wind causes the waves and you're the cause of the wind— THEN BLOW SOFTLY. 'Breeze' us to the promised land. We don't need to have a mountain wave crash over us ever. We'll sit on deck, we'll get suntans, we will fish, we will play shuffleboard. We will do a cruise to the promised land. Still the storms, calm the seas, rebuke the winds." Isn't that a wonderful solution?

Are there precedents for God stilling storms? We just referred to one. The night Jesus walked on the water he calmed the wind afterward, and the scripture specifically says: "And immediately the ship was at the land whither they went" (John 6:21). Isn't that the ideal finale to the crises of our lives? "Please calm my storms, Lord, and *immediately* get me to my destination." He can do it, can't he? When the storms are blowing in my life, that is usually the solution I desire—simply still the storm, at least still it in the second watch. But if we arrive at the darkness of the fourth watch and he hasn't stilled it, we likely have learned something—something wonderful and powerful, something about ourselves.

The next verse says: "Behold, *I prepare you* against these things; for ye cannot cross this great deep save *I prepare you* against the waves of the sea, and the winds which have gone forth, and the floods which shall come. Therefore what will ye that *I should prepare for you* that ye may have light when ye are swallowed up in the depths of the sea?" (Ether 2:25; emphasis added).

Given the choice between helping us by calming the storms or preparing us before they ever come, which do you think the Lord prefers? He's a fourth-watch God; he's also a tight-like-a-dish

God. If we arrive at the fourth watch and he has not come, what do we know about our ships? THEY ARE TIGHT LIKE A DISH. Our Father in Heaven already foresaw all the storms, complete with their mountain waves. He foresaw all the problems, all the disappointments and frustrations, the temptations, and trials of life; and before the wind ever started to blow, he prepared us to withstand it. We're not going to sink. We're going to be all right. Because if our ships weren't tight like a dish, and there was fear that the mountain waves would capsize or drown us, what would he do? He would still the storm. If he doesn't still the storm, if he doesn't come by the fourth watch, we know our vessels are tight like a dish.

I think that assurance is, in part, the meaning of a promise Isaiah made. Here are the Lord's comforting words: "And it shall come to pass, that before they call, I will answer; and while they are yet speaking, I will hear" (Isaiah 65:24). Before we ever call out to him in the storms, the Lord knew they would come, and He has prepared our vessels. We need not fear. We'll feel the promised land under our feet.

WHEN HE COMES IN
THE FIRST WATCH

THERE IS ONE AREA of our lives where the Lord is willing and anxious to come to us in the first watch. In fact, if the Lord said to us, *I will let you choose one part of your life where I will come to you in the first watch, or, if you would like me to, I will choose the area for you,* hopefully we would have the wisdom to say to him, *I'll trust your judgment. You choose the times in my life when you'll be a first-watch God for me.* That area would be in forgiveness. The Savior is anxious and eager to come to us when we cry to him for forgiveness, even in the first watch. When the pain and the trial we are going through is repentance, when we struggle with the agonies of guilt, then he is a first-watch God. That truth is attested to countless times in the scriptures.

One of my all-time favorite scripture stories is that of the Prodigal Son. Contained in that parable is a powerful "first-watch" example that shows the eagerness the Lord feels to forgive. "And when he came to himself, he said, How many hired servants of my father's have bread enough and to spare, and I perish with hunger! I will arise and go to my father, and will say unto him, Father, I have sinned against heaven, and before thee, and am no more worthy to be called thy son: make me as one of thy hired servants" (Luke 15:17–19).

This parable was given to answer a question, which can be stated as follows: "When I 'come to myself,' when I return, when I seek forgiveness, do I return as a son or a servant?" The prodigal himself felt unworthy to return as a son; he was content to return as a servant. Should he be for the rest of his life a kind of second-class citizen of the kingdom? The parable answers: "There are no servants in the kingdom, only sons." Here is our first-watch verse: "He arose, and came to his father. But when he was yet a great way off, his father saw him, and had compassion, and ran, and fell on his neck, and kissed him" (Luke 15:20).

Sometimes it is very important to get the tone of a scripture right. Should we read the son's next comment with a tone of confession or one of amazement? I prefer that of astonishment at the greeting he has just received from his father. "And the son said unto him, Father, I have sinned against heaven, and in thy sight, and am no more worthy to be called thy son" (Luke 15:21). We might add, "Why do you treat me as one?"

"But the father said to his servants, Bring forth the best robe, and put it on him; and put a ring on his hand, and shoes on his feet: and bring hither the fatted calf, and kill it; and let us eat, and be merry: For this my son was dead, and is alive again; he was lost, and is found" (Luke 15:22–24).

As we progress through the Book of Mormon we see a theme begin to emerge as we read story after story. Everybody in the Book of Mormon who asks for forgiveness receives it. And they receive it immediately. The book of Mosiah speaks of "the immediate goodness of God" (Mosiah 25:10), and Amulek promises the humble Zoramites that "the great plan of redemption" will be brought unto them "immediately" if their hearts are soft (Alma

34:31). It's as if the Lord says: *Maybe you won't receive that message if I only include it once or twice. Maybe you won't realize how important the message is, so I'm going to put it in again and again, so you'll realize when the wind that blows against you has to do with guilt and forgiveness and repentance and transgression, I will come to you in the first watch.*

We read in Enos: "There came a voice unto me, saying: Enos, thy sins are forgiven thee, and thou shalt be blessed. . . . And I said: Lord, how is it done? And he said unto me: Because of thy faith in Christ, whom thou hast never before heard nor seen" (Enos 1:5, 7–8). It's as though the Lord ponders: *I wonder if they understand clearly from Enos's example? Let's state it again with Benjamin's people.* And a few pages later, we read: "They all cried aloud with one voice, saying: O have mercy, and apply the atoning blood of Christ that we may receive forgiveness of our sins, and our hearts may be purified; . . . And it came to pass that after they had spoken these words the Spirit of the Lord came upon them, and they were filled with joy, having received a remission of their sins, and having peace of conscience" (Mosiah 4:2–3).

Perhaps the Lord reflects once more: *I wonder if they got the message. We'd better remind them again.* We turn a few more pages and come to Zeezrom, to whom Alma says: "If thou believest in the redemption of Christ thou canst be healed." To which Zeezrom answers, "Yea, I believe according to thy words. And then Alma cried, . . . O Lord our God, have mercy on this man, and heal him according to his faith which is in Christ. And when Alma had said these words, Zeezrom leaped upon his feet, and began to walk" (Alma 15:8–11).

As if the conviction is not yet deep enough in our hearts the Lord imprints it deeper with the story of Alma and the sons of Mosiah. In agony of guilt, Alma cries out: "O Jesus, thou Son of God, have mercy on me, who am in the gall of bitterness, and am encircled about by the everlasting chains of death. And now, behold, when I thought this, I could remember my pains no more; yea, I was harrowed up by the memory of my sins no more. And oh, what joy, and what marvelous light I did behold" (Alma 36:18–20).

Are we convinced yet? In case we need more evidence we next turn to the Lamanites. *Include the*

prayers of Lamoni and his wife, the Lord whispers to
Mormon as he collects from the many records
those chosen few needed for the latter-day world.
Lamoni prays: "O Lord, have mercy; according to
thy abundant mercy which thou hast had upon the
people of Nephi, have upon me, and my people"
(Alma 18:41). When Lamoni revives from his little
sleep, he testifies, "As sure as thou livest, behold, I
have seen my Redeemer; and he shall come forth,
and be born of a woman, and he shall redeem all
mankind who believe on his name" (Alma 19:13).
Then Lamoni's wife, a short time later, adds her
witness to the growing list: "O blessed Jesus, who
has saved me from an awful hell! O blessed God,
have mercy on this people!" (Alma 19:29).
Lamoni's father receives forgiveness, and Lamoni's
servants also understand the "immediate goodness"
of our Savior.

Even the Lamanites who had come into the
prison to kill Nephi and Lehi were "filled with that
joy which is unspeakable and full of glory. . . . And
it came to pass that there came a voice unto them,
yea, a pleasant voice, as if it were a whisper, saying:

Peace, peace be unto you, because of your faith in my Well Beloved, who was from the foundation of the world" (Helaman 5:44–47). When we yearn for forgiveness, we worship a first-watch God.

I have emphasized the Savior's willingness to come to us in the first watch when it regards the forgiveness of our sins and transgressions. Of course this implies that we have done all we can do on our part to be worthy of that level of mercy. In Alma 24, the Anti-Nephi-Lehies refer to themselves as the "most lost of all mankind." But the Savior's mercy covered even them. It should be noted, however, that we read three times in that chapter that the Anti-Nephi-Lehies did "all [they] could do to repent sufficiently" (Alma 24:11–15). If we are willing to do as much as we can do, even though we may consider ourselves the most lost of all mankind, the Savior will come to us in the first watch, and we will know by experience the meaning of the words, "the immediate goodness of God."

Jesus instructed his disciples to forgive their brothers when they repented and asked for forgiveness. Then he added the following, "And if he trespass against thee seven times in a day, and seven times in a day turn again to thee, saying, I repent; thou shalt forgive him" (Luke 17:4). I do not believe the Lord is going to expect of us a higher standard than he himself is willing to give. If, therefore, he anticipates we will forgive one another when repentance is offered, seven times in a day, surely that means he will abide by an equal if not a greater standard. Let us do all that we can do, then with full assurance, with a confidence born of hope engendered by the Savior's many examples, we may go to him seven times in a single day and know that every time we will hear the words, "I forgive you. Go in peace."

HOLDING PLACES
OF THE HEART

OCCASIONALLY, ANSWERS aren't given or the blessings we desire don't come or the trials we bear continue because there is no place in our hearts for God to put the answer we need. Life must carve or hollow out this place. The very experiences we are going through help to create these holding places. Yet he still hears our prayers and promises the resolution will come in time.

When the Missouri persecutions were raging, the Lord comforted the Saints by telling them: "Fear not, let your hearts be comforted; yea, rejoice evermore, and in everything give thanks; waiting patiently on the Lord, for your prayers have entered into the ears of the Lord of Sabaoth, and are recorded with this seal and testament—the Lord hath sworn and decreed that they shall be granted" (D&C 98:1–2). Not yet, nevertheless they will be granted. "He giveth this promise unto you, with an immutable covenant that they shall be ful-filled; and all things wherewith you have been afflicted shall work together for your good, and to my name's glory" (D&C 98:3).

Moses once asked the Lord a question after having been shown the multitude of God's cre-ations. *Why do you create all these wonders?* he puzzled. The Lord answered, *I have my reasons.* These are his words: "For mine own purpose have I made these things. Here is wisdom and it remaineth in me" (Moses 1:31). Now that's a very polite way of say-ing, *I'm not going to answer your question, Moses. You want to know why I create all these things? I have a purpose and it's a wise purpose, but I'm not going to make it known to you right now.* We know that God eventually answered Moses' question. The answer is a very famous one: "This is my work and my glory—to bring to pass the immortality and eternal life of man" (Moses 1:39). *I create all these worlds to make men gods,* the Lord was saying. I have often asked myself why the Lord didn't answer Moses when he initially asked the question. A close reading reveals that God wanted Moses to understand a few things before the answer came—things that would make the answer even more powerful. He was creating a holding place in Moses' heart to receive it.

Let me illustrate this particular concept by a personal story. When I was just a baby, my father, because of concerns in his own life and challenges that he was having, left our family. Our mother alone, therefore, raised my sisters and me, and as I was growing up, my father had very little to do with us as children. I realize he was working with things in his own life, but his decisions created certain challenges and hardships for my mother, my sisters, and for me. At age fourteen or fifteen, if you were in my situation, and you knelt down and said: "Father in Heaven, help me find peace concerning my father leaving us and really having nothing to do with us for all these years. Help me forgive my father," would you not think that was an appropriate prayer, one that deserved an answer? But no answer came at age fourteen and fifteen. Twenty, twenty-one comes, same prayers, still no answer. Twenty-five, twenty-six passes, same prayers, yet still no answer. Thirty, thirty-one, thirty-three, thirty-four all come and go. Surely I'm in the fourth watch by now, would you not agree?

Then one day I was asked to prepare a talk on families. I thought I would speak about my mother. My mother was a saint. In my eyes she could do no wrong. I would talk about my mother—her wisdom and goodness, and how she raised us. But the Spirit seemed to whisper, *Speak about your father.* And I thought, *What am I going to say about my father? I have hardly had anything to do with my father growing up.* Yet the Spirit seemed to urge that I think about him.

Just at that moment, my two sons came into the room where I was working. I was married, and I had two daughters and two sons at the time. The eldest son was about six, his younger brother was around two, and they stood in front of me, just stood there staring at me. I looked at my boys and all at once the Spirit literally flooded my mind with wonderful memories of things that I had shared with them.

We are told that a whole life can pass before us just before we die and we see everything all at once. It was that kind of experience. All the simple little memories, none of them major, came into focus—carving Halloween pumpkins; trick-or-treating with bags bulging with candy; Christmas mornings and the aroma of gingerbread; listening to their tiny-voice prayers; their first tearful, hesitant Primary talks; a squirming puppy wrapped in the tangle of their arms; walks by the pond to see the turtles; piggy-back rides; reading stories at night with mimicked voices; catching a fish out of the same hole where I caught my first fish twenty-five years earlier; the smell of saddle leather as I lifted them for their first horseback ride. All these simple, tiny, little, everyday memories that I shared in those years with my sons washed into my soul.

And then the Spirit said: *I am now ready to answer your question. Now that you are a father, now that you know a father's love, would you be the son who lost his father, or the father who lost his son?* When I heard those words, I just began to weep. I grabbed my sons and hugged them and just sobbed and sobbed.

My wife came into the room; I was holding those two boys and crying. Not for *me!* For *my father!* Because I knew what he had missed. He doesn't know what he missed. There's a mercy in that. But I knew what he missed, and I knew it was a greater tragedy to be the father who lost his son than to be the son who lost a father.

My wife became concerned and said, "For heaven's sake, Mike, what is the matter?" I said, "I can't talk about it now." I went up and shut myself in the bathroom and cried myself dry. Have you ever done that? There are no tears coming—you're still crying, and there's nothing coming?

Why didn't my Father in Heaven give me that answer at fifteen, or twenty-one, or twenty-five, or when I was married, or when my daughters were born? He needed to wait until I was a father of sons and had enough experiences with my boys to understand what a sweet thing it is to be a father and share memories with sons. The holding place had to be carved in my heart, and as soon as I could really receive and comprehend the answer, the Lord gave it to me. Maybe we are in the fourth watch, but the Lord is saying to us: *I'll answer your prayer. I'm aware of your needs. It is recorded in heaven, and I'm going to answer it. But right now in your life there's no place for me to put the answer. Life will create a holding place, and as soon as you are able to receive it, I will give it to you.*

STONES
OR BREAD

THERE ARE TIMES in my life when I think He answers, but I misunderstand the message. I think I'm in the fourth watch, but I'm really not; it's just that I expected one answer and got another. In the Gospel of Luke the Lord urges us to come to him for answers: "Ask," he says, "and it shall be given you; seek, and ye shall find; knock, and it shall be opened unto you." (He is always telling us that. It's one of those principles he repeats many, many times because he does not want us to miss it.) "For every one that asketh receiveth; and he that seeketh findeth; and to him that knocketh it shall be opened" (Luke 11:9–10).

He then illustrates that truth: "If a son shall ask bread of any of you that is a father, will he give him a stone? or if he ask a fish, will he for a fish give him a serpent? Or if he shall ask an egg, will he offer him a scorpion? If ye then, being evil [meaning being human—imperfect], know how to give good gifts unto your children: how much more shall your heavenly Father give [good gifts through] the Holy Spirit to them that ask him?" (Luke 11:11–13).

There are times in our lives when I think the Lord says, *I gave you bread, but it wasn't the kind of bread you wanted and because you keep thinking about the kind of bread you wanted you've turned my bread into a stone. I gave you a fish, but it wasn't the flavor of fish that you wanted, and you've turned the fish into a serpent. Or I gave you an egg, but I cooked it differently from how you ordered it, and you think I've given you a scorpion.*

C. S. Lewis speaks of two kinds of good—the *expected* good and the *given* good. All things given from God are good. There are times in my life I have to remind myself God does not give stones, and when we need bread, a stone is something useless. God does not give stones—only bread. God does not give serpents or scorpions—they are harmful things. He only gives eggs and fish. But if I'm not careful I may hatch the scorpion out of the egg; I may interpret the given good as something bad by constantly thinking of what I wanted instead of what I received. Does that make some kind of sense?

Let me give you an illustration. When I was young I wanted to go on a mission. I dreamed of that mission. I thought I should learn a language, so I took French starting in the eighth grade. I took it in the ninth grade, the tenth grade, and the eleventh grade. I quit after the eleventh grade because I didn't like the French teacher. She was from Paris, was very proud of her language, and if you mispronounced a word (for instance the French "R," which is rather difficult for an American to get right), she would throw chalk at you. She would literally pelt you with chalk. If you really insulted her ears by butchering her language, she would throw an eraser at you. And I got pelted quite a bit. I thought, *If this is what the French are like, the last place on earth I want to go on a mission is France.* Besides, I loved all things Danish—I'm half Danish. My mother would tell you the good half of me is the Danish half. My grandfather went to Denmark, my uncles went to Denmark, my cousins went to

Denmark. It was tradition in the family for the boys to go to Denmark on their missions. I wanted to go to Denmark, wanted it as much as I have ever wanted anything. I wanted to do Danish research in family history. I figured the Lord would recognize my need to go to Denmark. I prayed I would go to Denmark. But I had the feeling of impending doom that I was not going to go to Denmark—I was going to go to France. So I began to plead with the Lord that he would send me to Denmark. I prayed night after night for a Danish mission.

As the bishop and I began to fill out the missionary papers, I had a feeling it probably was not appropriate to tell the Lord which country he should send you for your mission, but I didn't think it was inappropriate to eliminate one country out of the hundreds in the world. I changed my prayers. I began to pray he would send me anywhere but France.

I remember vividly the day my call arrived. I was at work. I knew it was at home. Nobody notified me; I just knew the call was waiting for me in the mailbox. We've all seen the videos of the excited missionary who runs home and opens the letter, complete with the accompanying jubilation. I knew my call was in the mailbox, and I knew it said France. Don't ask me how I knew, I just did. I did not want to go home and open it. I lingered at work until the last moment. I was so discouraged over the fact that I was going to France that I actually—and you're going to think I am making this up, but I actually did this (I'm eighteen—you'd think an eighteen-year-old would have more sense)—I pulled to the side of the road, parked the car, bowed my head, and said, "Father in Heaven, I know my call is at home, I know it says France. Thou art all-powerful! Thou canst do all things! Please change it in the envelope. I will go anywhere, I don't need to go to Denmark, I will go anywhere, just please, please don't send me to France!"

I ended my prayer, drove home with a spark of hope, and opened the envelope. What did it say? France. Actually, I sometimes think that originally it said Denmark, and the Lord looked down and said, *We really need to teach this young man something, so let's change it in the envelope. He needs to go to France.*

So I went to France. Now I could have ruined my mission. The *expected* good was Denmark. Or, after a while, any place on earth. That was the expected good. The *given* good was France. It didn't take me very long in France to love the French people. I love the French people—wonderful people. They have a beautiful language. Their culture went right to the center of my heart. I had a marvelous mission. We were successful. I found out later, when I returned home, that I had French ancestors, some of them living in the very cities and areas I had served in. I didn't know that at the time, but the Lord did.

I repeat, all things given of God are good. He doesn't give scorpions; he only gives eggs. He does not give stones; he only gives bread. Whatever he gives is good!

That is true of callings. When we moved to Utah about twenty years ago, I hoped I could be the Gospel Doctrine teacher. My favorite calling in the church is Gospel Doctrine. I love to teach the scriptures—it's rewarding, tremendous fun. We'd been in the ward only a few months and, lo and behold, they released the Gospel Doctrine teacher!

That afternoon the bishop asked me to come with my wife to his office to receive a calling. Well, I *knew* it was going to be Gospel Doctrine—this is an inspired church, this bishop was called of God— obviously he would have seen that I need to be the Gospel Doctrine teacher.

I sat down, and he said, "Brother Wilcox, we have a call for you. We would like you to teach the deacons, to be the deacons quorum advisor." My first response was (I didn't say it, but I was thinking it), *Who called you to be a bishop? I work with college kids. What language do deacons speak? I don't speak deacon.* But as the good member, like all of you would do, I said, "Thank you for the call. I would be very happy to teach the deacons." I went home and said to my wife, "Oh, I thought this was an inspired Church."

Could I have ruined that call? I could have if I kept thinking every Sunday: *I should be teaching Gospel Doctrine.* That would have made it a miserable call, but I got to really love those little guys, and the Lord helped me the first Sunday when I went into the classroom and, so to speak, met the enemy. The Spirit just whispered, *Teach them well. One day one of them might be your son-in-law.* I had daughters who were deacon age and just under deacon age. My daughters didn't marry any of those boys, but I think the Lord was saying that somewhere, someplace there is a deacon who will be your son-in-law—teach these boys as well as you hope another advisor is teaching his boys.

I had a wonderful experience with the deacons. You can call me to be the deacons quorum advisor any time and I will celebrate. God did not give me stones; he gave me bread in all of those moments.

NOT
THIS WAY

SOMETIMES THE ANSWER we receive is simply: *No, not this way.* When the Lord gives that kind of answer, our impatience sometimes causes us to say, *Well, then, which way do you want me to go?* I've always been intrigued with Paul's second missionary journey. If you look at it on the map, he's crossing Turkey, Asia Minor, in a very logical, methodical way—east toward west, south toward north. It's very logical. We read in Acts: "They had gone throughout Phrygia and the region of Galatia" (Acts 16:6). Now, if you look at the map the very next logical spot for Paul to preach the gospel would be Ephesus in Asia; that's logical, and that's where he was headed. But we read, "[They] were forbidden of the Holy Ghost to preach the word in Asia." *Okay, you don't want me to preach in Ephesus, so I'll go to the north instead of the west of Turkey, to a place called Bithynia.*

They tried to go into Bithynia, but the Spirit "suffered them not. And they passing by Mysia came down to Troas. And a vision appeared to Paul in the night; There stood a man of Macedonia, and prayed him, saying, Come over into Macedonia, and help us" (Acts 16:7–9). Responding to his vision, Paul skips Ephesus and jumps to Greece where he establishes churches in Thessalonica, Philippi, Athens, and Corinth before the Spirit allows him to go back to Turkey and preach in Ephesus. Paul does a backward circle, and the Lord never tells us in the scriptures why he didn't want Paul to preach in Ephesus at that time.

Notice, however, how the instructions came. The Lord didn't say, *Paul, would you go over to Corinth? I want you there.* It was instead, *No, not this way.* And sometimes the Lord in our lives says, *No, not this way.* Far too often our response is, *Well, then, which way?* but he doesn't always specify it. Then we try another way. *No, not this way,* comes the answer. Eventually we receive the vision and know where we're supposed to go, but there is some trial and error involved in the process. We must be patient. The Lord knows what he is doing.

THE POOREST
SOIL

W HILE WE ARE WAITING for the fourth watch there is always hope even in the most desperate situations or trials. I was at a "Time Out for Women" event a few years ago, and one of the other speakers was conducting a question-and-answer session with the women who were there. One of the sisters asked a series of questions that resonated with many of the other women gathered on that occasion. I could tell by the response of the audience. The questions were: "Why did my life not turn out like I thought it would when I was young?" "Why does it seem that everything in my life goes wrong?" "I get trial after trial after trial and, yet, when I look at other sisters, their lives seem to be going so smoothly. How come my life can't go smoothly like their lives? I recognize that I don't know all they are going through and, yet, so many of my expectations have failed to appear and some of my worst fears have come. Why?"

I listened to those questions and thought of my own life. Her life turned out, we might say, worse than expected, and I thought, *My life's turned out better than I anticipated. God has been very kind to me.* Maybe that is so because I didn't expect a great deal when I was young and received so much more. It's made me believe that when you don't expect a lot from life and you obtain so many blessings, the natural result is gratitude, and that is an emotion that is wonderful to feel. She had touched some of my deepest sympathies, and I wondered about the fairness of life with a twinge of guilt as I reflected on my own. *She was living such a difficult life while others seem to have such a good life. Why doesn't God help her in ways that he has helped others?*

I found an answer in the Book of Mormon and turned to it as I sat in the auditorium reflecting on her situation. In the allegory of the tame and the wild olive tree we find an encouraging truth. I like to read Jacob 5 not as an allegory, but as a parable—a parable that is designed to teach us some important things about life. We could call it the Parable of the Good Vineyard Owner. Notice this section of that story as it applies to that concerned woman's questions and her experiences with life.

The Lord of the vineyard accompanied by his servant is making the rounds of the vineyard, surveying the different branches of the original tree that he scattered. Remember, he had taken the tender branches and planted them in different spots of his vineyard. They have been growing for a while, and it's time to check their progress, to monitor their growth. This time as we read the story let us think of the trees as individual people trying to grow and progress as best they can while here on the earth.

The Lord visits the first tree and says: "Behold these; and he beheld the first that it had brought forth much fruit; and he beheld also that it was good. And he said unto the servant: Take of the fruit thereof, and lay it up against the season, that I may preserve it unto mine own self; for behold, said he, this long time have I nourished it, and it hath brought forth much fruit" (Jacob 5:20).

The servant then asks the master something that we all often ask the Lord in one way or another. When I look toward heaven and cry: "Did heaven look on, and would not take their part?" I try to remember this part of the allegory. It is comforting. The servant said: "How comest thou hither to plant this tree, or this branch of the tree? For behold, it was *the poorest spot in all the land of thy vineyard*" (Jacob 5:21; emphasis added). Now that's what that good sister was asking, isn't it? She was saying, *Why did I get planted in the poor spot of the vineyard?*

My heart echoed her question: *Yes, Lord, that's a good question. Why did she get planted in the poorest spot of the vineyard, because I know a lot more poor-spot-of-the-vineyard people who are wondering the same thing.* We all know poor-spot-of-the-vineyard people. Maybe we think we are a poor-spot-of-the-vineyard person; and we may be right.

The Lord of the vineyard answered his servant and said unto him; "Counsel me not" (Jacob 5:22). In other words, *I know what I'm doing in my vineyard.* It is sometimes so very difficult not to give in to the temptation to counsel the Lord on his running of the world, especially as it concerns our own lives.

But we get some information in the Lord's comments that I think is comforting, certainly for those who are in the poorer spots of the vineyard or have reached the fourth watch and wonder why the wind is still blowing. The Lord replies: "*I knew that it was a poor spot of ground*" (Jacob 5:22; emphasis added). That's comforting—he knows! *I know the situation in your life isn't the best,* he whispers to us, *I know that.* We don't need to try to pretend things are really better than they are, to live an illusory, put-your-best-face-forward satisfaction or happiness. That does not mean we don't count our blessings or that we just give up and sink into despair, but it does mean the Lord is aware in a very honest way that our soil isn't as ideal as we both would like it to be.

Notice then the Lord's next comment: "Wherefore, I said unto thee, *I have nourished it this long time*" (Jacob 5:22; emphasis added). That's the second piece of information he deeply desires us to comprehend. *I know it's a poor spot, so I have nourished it a long time. I have not left you to fare as best you can in a difficult situation.* A lot of nourishing has been going on, much of it in ways that are challenging for a mortal to understand, but it is there nonetheless.

A third thing he wants us to understand about life in the vineyard is contained in his next words to the servant: "Thou beholdest *that it hath brought forth much fruit*" (Jacob 5:22; emphasis added). Even in the poorest spots of ground, good fruit can be produced because of the nourishment God has provided. These are the fruits of character, nobility, patience, compassion, empathy, and godliness, even genius, all of which have and will continue to rise out of some of the most debilitating of soils. Then the Lord of the vineyard calls our attention to another tree, saying, "Look hither; behold I have planted another branch of the tree also; and thou knowest that this spot of ground *was poorer than the first*" (Jacob 5:23; emphasis added). That's the fourth thing he wants us to recognize. There are others who are in even a poorer situation than the one we find ourselves in. That may be poor comfort, but it is effective nonetheless. What does he do for them? His words to his servant reveal this. "But, behold the tree. I have nourished it this long time, and *it hath brought forth much fruit*" (Jacob 5:23;

emphasis added). I sense a slight tone of righteous pride in the Lord's words, "But, behold the tree." Even in the poorest of the poor spots of ground, God can bring forth good fruit.

Then, almost as if to seal the principle, he says to the servant: "Look hither, and behold the last. Behold, this have I planted in a good spot of ground" (Jacob 5:25). What kind of fruit would we foresee growing from this last spot of good ground? Since the soil is so rich, would it not be anticipated that the fruits would be comparable? The best fruit produced from the best ground? Yet we read: "I have nourished it this long time, and only a part of the tree hath brought forth tame fruit, and the other part of the tree hath brought forth wild fruit; behold, I have nourished this tree like unto the others" (Jacob 5:25).

It isn't the spot of ground we're planted in that matters; it's how we respond to the Lord's nourishing. The poorest of the poor spots of ground can bring forth some of the sweetest fruits. We must believe this or else we will allow our circumstances and environment to determine our lives and the quality of our souls.

THE GREATNESS
OF GOD

WE CAN ALSO FIND COMFORT in the knowledge that God will turn all things in our life to good. This is a principle that is taught often in the scriptures. No situation is ever negative in the long run and, therefore, life is always fair. Whatever happens to us God can turn it to good if we trust him and stay on the path. He teaches that principle in every book of scripture. In the Book of Mormon, Lehi testifies to his son Jacob: "In thy childhood thou hast suffered afflictions and much sorrow, because of the rudeness of thy brethren. Nevertheless, Jacob, my firstborn in the wilderness, *thou knowest the greatness of God; and he shall consecrate thine afflictions for thy gain* (2 Nephi 2:1–2; emphasis added). Part of God's greatness consists in his ability to turn even the most negative of situations into positive truth and learning.

The Lord instructed Joseph Smith in this principle while the Prophet was suffering in Liberty Jail. We can all quote this one: "All these things shall give thee experience, and shall be for thy good" (D&C 122:7). Paul, who also suffered a great deal, bore witness: "We know that all things work together for good to them that love God" (Romans 8:28). Joseph in the Old Testament named his two sons Manasseh and Ephraim, in a manner that teaches the principle. *Manasseh* means "forgetting," and *Ephraim* means "fruitful." As he named his two boys, Joseph said: "God . . . hath made me forget all my toil, and . . . hath caused me to be fruitful in the land of my affliction" (Genesis 41:51–52). Our Father in Heaven can turn even the most negative situations to good for us, if we will trust him and stay true to his gospel.

C. S. Lewis once wrote a little piece that very poignantly taught this truth. He said:

> Ye cannot in your present state understand eternity. . . . But ye can get some likeness of it if ye say

that both good and evil, when they are full grown, become retrospective. . . . All their earthly past will have been Heaven to those who are saved. . . . All their life on Earth too, will then be seen by the damned to have been Hell. That is what mortals misunderstand. They say of some temporal suffering, "No future bliss can make up for it," not knowing that Heaven, once attained, will work backwards and turn even that agony into a glory. And of some sinful pleasure they say "Let me have but *this* and I'll take the consequences": little dreaming how damnation will spread back and back into their past and contaminate the pleasure of the sin. Both processes begin even before death. The good man's past begins to change so that his forgiven sins and remembered sorrows take on the quality of Heaven: the bad man's past already conforms to his badness and is filled only with dreariness. And that is why, at the end of all things, when the sun rises here and the twilight turns to blackness down there, the Blessed will say, "We have never lived anywhere except in Heaven," and the Lost, "We were always in Hell." And both will speak truly (*The Great Divorce* [San Francisco: HarperCollins, 2001], 69; italics in original).

WIPE AWAY ALL TEARS

WE ALSO ARE PROMISED by the Lord that all sorrows, trials, all storms, all fourth, ninth, or tenth watches will one day end. When I served as a bishop I soon discovered that the main purpose of a bishop was to hand out tissues. It didn't take me very long to realize that I would see a lot of tears in my five years of service. I would always carry tissues—I still do. I always have them in my pockets, because on any given Sunday I would see tears—tears of sorrow over the death of loved ones, tears of guilt in confession, tears of children over the divorce of parents, tears of parents over rebellious children, tears of wives over inactive husbands, tears of old, tired bodies longing for death—so many different kinds of tears. I would hand them a tissue and watch them wipe the tears from their cheeks. I became very frustrated because I wanted to help them wipe the tears off their souls, not just off their faces. Then one day I came across a beautiful verse in the Book of Revelation, a promise God makes to all of us. This is what he assures us: "God shall wipe away all tears from their eyes; and there shall be no more death, neither sorrow, nor crying, neither shall there be any more pain: for the former things are passed away" (Revelation 21:4). That is promised twice in the Book of Revelation and originally in Isaiah. I realized at that moment, though I as a bishop could not wipe away the tears, there was One who could do so. One day he will do so. He will wipe away all tears.

That's an intimate image. He didn't say, *I will hand them a tissue.* He said, *I'll wipe the tears away.* When I think of my own experiences, who has ever wiped tears from my eyes? My mother, my wife, maybe a child, but only in the most intimate and deepest of relationships would one dare to reach out a gentle thumb and sweep it across the cheek to wipe away a tear. Yet the promise is that the Lord will do that for us all.

In the New Testament the Lord then reminds us of one of his titles: "I am Alpha and Omega, *the beginning and the end*" (Revelation 21:6; emphasis added). If we take that title, given in the context of wiping away all tears, and apply it to the promise, and then ask the question, *What is He the end of?* we learn a marvelous truth. He answers us: *I am the end of death, I am the end of crying, I am the end of sorrow, I am the end of pain.* Now if we ask the question, *What is he the beginning of?* He will answer: *I am the beginning of peace, I am the beginning of forgiveness, I am the beginning of life and happiness and glory. I am the beginning of all joys.*

One day, no matter what reason we may have for unhappiness; whatever trial we may face, have faced, or are then facing; one day they will all come to an end. Right at the end of his agonies on the cross, Jesus said, "It is finished." He certainly meant that his Father's will had completely been accomplished, but there is something more in those simple words. His *suffering* was also over. No man suffered more than he did, and if *he* came to a point in his life where he could say of his suffering, "It is finished," all of *us* will come to the point in our existence when we, too, will say, "It is finished."

And it will be finished, no matter what it was. The tears will be wiped away. That end we may hope for. That end we may be assured of. In the meantime we may know that whatever happens he is going to turn it into good for us. So let the fourth watches come. Let the mountain waves crash. Life will be sweet eventually.

THE BURNING BUSH

I HAVE LONG LOVED the story of God's appearance to Moses in the burning bush. I think it is a wonderful image to hold on to when we think of our Father in Heaven: "Now Moses kept the flock of Jethro his father in law, the priest of Midian: and he led the flock to the backside of the desert, and came to the mountain of God, even to Horeb. And the angel of the Lord appeared unto him in a flame of fire out of the midst of a bush: and he looked, and, behold, *the bush burned with fire, and the bush was not consumed.* And Moses said, I will now turn aside, and see this great sight, why the bush is not burnt" (Exodus 3:1–3; emphasis added).

It is so very critical to believe, and to believe firmly, that God is a burning fire that is unique above all other fires. He will give us warmth! He will give us light! He will cleanse and purge us as does the refiner's fire! But he will not consume us. The flame of his love is meant only for good—it is not a destroying fire. Of this we may be certain. "The bush was not consumed," nor will we be in our encounters with the God of Light.

I conclude with this final thought. I believe every good thing in life that we desire is on the strait and narrow path. As long as we stay on the path every truly enjoyable and fine thing life and eternity can offer will be ours. Sometimes, while seeking for happiness or fulfillment we may stray from the path, vainly believing we will find our hearts' desires beyond the road our Savior has established, but if we'll stay on the path, everything we want in life will be ours. It's a wish-fulfilling path designed to lead us to every good, noble, righteous thing we want, if we'll just follow it. In truth it will provide greater things than we can even imagine, for did not the Lord say: "Since the beginning of the world men have not heard, nor perceived by the ear, neither hath the eye seen, O God, beside thee, what he hath prepared for him that waiteth for him" (Isaiah 64:4).

If you are like me, I usually want the desirable blessing to be just a few feet ahead of me on the path. However, sometimes the Lord has to give me a pair of binoculars and say, *Well, it's on the path, but it's in the distance there.* Then I must be patient, confident that if I'll just walk the path, all will, in due time, be well.

May we walk that path, trusting that every desire of our hearts that truly brings happiness, will be there. May God bless us in our fourth watches. May our ships be tight like a dish. May we have the patience to wait for life, measured by the wisdom of God, to carve the holding places in our hearts. May we remember God does not give stones or serpents, he only gives bread and fish. May we understand all things God gives are good, and even the negative ones he can make good. May we respond to his nourishing and bring forth good fruit in spite of the soil in which we may have been planted. May we trust that the Lord himself will in time wipe away all tears. May God's burning fire give us warmth, light, and cleansing. And may the Lord bless us as we walk his path of happiness.

This is my prayer for myself, my family, my friends, and for all of God's children wherever they may be.